Welcome to
an ILLUSTRATED WORLD TOUR

© 2021 Instituto Monsa de ediciones.

First edition in November 2021 by Monsa Publications,
Gravina 43 (08930) Sant Adrià de Besós.
Barcelona (Spain) T +34 93 381 00 93
www.monsa.com monsa@monsa.com

Editor and Project Director Anna Minguet
Design, layout, text editing Eva Minguet
(Monsa Publications)
Translation Somostraductores.com
Printing Cachiman Gráfic

Shop online: www.monsashop.com
Follow us!: Instagram: @monsapublications

ISBN: 978-84-17557-43-0
D.L. B 17327-2021
November 2021

Image credits: amisb©123rf, anastasiiakurman©123rf, balabolka©123rf, brillianata©123rf, captainvector©123rf, coffeeein©123rf, cookamoto©123rf, chukchuk©123rf, darialazykova©123rf, ekaterinakapranova©123rf, elinkim©123rf, elizavetamelentyeva©123rf, goodstudio©123rf, gropgrop©123rf, hstrongart©123rf, incomible©123rf, irinakogan©123rf, ikeskinen©123rf, keltmd©123rf, kchung©123rf, knstart©123rf, klavapuk©123rf, liudmylaklymenko©123rf, macrovector©123rf, marish©123rf, maryianestsiarovich©123rf, moloko88©123rf, muchmaniavector©123rf, nataliachernyshova©123rf, natashapankina©123rf, nickvector©123rf, olgazakharova©123rf, oksanastepova©123rf, svetlanagonchar©123rf, snapgalleria©123rf, stockillustration©123rf, seita©123rf, tatianahryn©123rf, tettygreen©123rf, vladimiryudin©123rf, vifromhell©123rf.

Welcome to
an ILLUSTRATED WORLD TOUR

PASSPORT

A12
A 12
G7 12:01

monsa

Intro

Traveling is synonymous with joy, fun, laughter, knowledge... Let yourself be carried away by the magic of illustrated maps created to show unique details of each place such as its cuisine, music and dance, traditions, architecture, sports, art... Because we believe that traveling is one of the best things we can do!

We travel because...

...getting out of our daily routine and getting to know different places frees us.
...getting to know people from other cultures and their ways of life are key to opening our minds and enriching ourselves.
...it is a pleasure to taste the traditional food of the place you are visiting, and to appreciate the variety and richness of the local cuisine.
...when you enjoy art, you can learn about the history of each city.
...it allows us to reach those dreamed of places.
...every trip will be a lifetime memory.

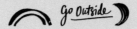

Viajar es alegría, diversión, risas, conocimiento... Déjate llevar por la magia de los mapas ilustrados, creados para mostrar detalles únicos de cada lugar, como su gastronomía, música y baile, tradiciones, arquitectura, deportes, arte... Porque creemos que viajar... ¡es una de las mejores cosas que podemos hacer!

Viajamos porque...

...salir de nuestra rutina diaria, conociendo lugares diferentes, nos libera.
...conocer personas de otras culturas y sus maneras de vivir, son claves para abrir nuestra mente y enriquecernos.
...es un placer probar las comidas típicas del sitio que estás visitando, y valorar la variedad y la riqueza de la gastronomía del lugar.
...disfrutando del arte, se puede conocer la historia de cada ciudad.
...nos permite llegar a aquellos lugares soñados.
...cada viaje será un recuerdo para toda la vida.

Welcome to Europe!

- Europe owes its name to the Phoenician princess Europa.
- More than 200 languages are spoken.
- There are more UNESCO World Heritage Sites in Europe than on any other continent in the world.
- Although Europeans identify themselves as such, they also have their own national and regional identities. Europe has some of the best preserved cultures and traditions in the world.
- More than 50% of the world's chocolate production is sold and consumed by Europeans.
- The Perućica Forest , in Bosnia-Herzegovina, is the last primeval forest in Europe.
- The Vatican is the smallest country in the world and home to the Pope.

- Debe su nombre a la princesa fenicia Europa.
- Se hablan más de 200 idiomas.
- Hay más sitios Patrimonio de la Humanidad de la UNESCO en Europa que en cualquier otro continente del mundo.
- Aunque los europeos se identifican a sí mismos como tal, también tienen su propia identidad nacional y regional. Europa tiene algunas de las culturas y tradiciones mejor conservadas del mundo.
- Más del 50 % de la producción mundial de chocolate es vendida y consumida por europeos.
- La selva de Perućica, en Bosnia-Herzegovina, es la última selva de Europa.
- El Vaticano es el país más pequeño del mundo y hogar del Papa.

Portugal
Olá!

CAPITAL
Lisbon

MUSIC AND TRADITIONAL DANCE
Fado and Corridinho

FOOD
Feijoada à transmontana, Sarrabulho papas, Ouos Moles, Queijo to Serra, and Caldereirada de Peixe

SPORT
Soccer, Athletics and Canoeing

TOP 5 FAMOUS ATTRACTIONS
Belém Tower, Pena Palace, Convento do Cristo, Castelo de Sao Jorge and Cliffs of Lagos

FRANCE

SANTIAGO DE
COMPOSTELA

HOLA

BARCELONA

PORTUGAL

MADRID

PALMA DE
MALLORCA

SEVILLA

MALAGA

SHERRY

SPAIN

Spain
¡Hola!

CAPITAL
Madrid

MUSIC AND TRADITIONAL DANCE
Flamenco

FOOD
Paella, Gazpacho and salmorejo, Potato
Omelette, Iberian Ham, Asturian Fabada, Galician
Octopus, Bravas Potatoes, Pisto, Calçots, Fried
Fish, Cachopo, Marmitako, Catalan Cream and
Churros with Chocolate

SPORT
Soccer, Tennis and Basketball

TOP 5 FAMOUS ATTRACTIONS
The Alhambra of Granada, Burgos Cathedral,
The Sagrada Familia of Barcelona, The Cordoba's
mosque and The Cathedral of Santiago

PARIS

France
Bonjour!

CAPITAL
Paris

MUSIC AND TRADITIONAL DANCE
Chanson Française, Can-Can, the Accordion and the Piano

FOOD
Raclette, Ratatouille, Foie Gras, Escargot, Quiche, Steak Tartare, Cheese Soufflé, Crêpe and Croissant

SPORT
Cycling, Soccer and Handball

TOP 5 FAMOUS ATTRACTIONS
Eiffel Tower, Arch of Triumph, Notre-Dame, Mont Saint-Michel and Castles of the Loire Valley

Italy
Ciao!

CAPITAL
Rome

MUSIC AND TRADITIONAL DANCE
Opera and Tarantella

FOOD
Pasta, Pizza, Risotto, Ossobuco, Tiramisù, Panna Cotta and Gelato

SPORT
Soccer, Auto Racing and Basketball

TOP 5 FAMOUS ATTRACTIONS
The Colosseum, The Trevi Fountain, The Leaning Tower, The Duomo and The Basilica of San Marco

Greece

Athens

Rhodes

Crete

Greece
Geia sou!

CAPITAL
Athens

MUSIC AND TRADITIONAL DANCE
Rebetiko and Sirtak

FOOD
Horiatiki, Tzaziki, Dolmadakia, Musaka, Souvlaki,
Loukoumades and Baklava

SPORT
Soccer, Basketball and Athletics

TOP 5 FAMOUS ATTRACTIONS
Acropolis of Athens, Temple of Apollo, Meteora
"the monasteries suspended from the sky",
Theater of Epidaurus and Poseidon's Temple

Turkey
Merhaba!

CAPITAL
Ankara

MUSIC AND TRADITIONAL DANCE
Koşma, Semai, Horon, Kaşık Oyunu, Kılıç Kalkan
and Zeybek

FOOD
Döner, Kuzu Tandır, Pilav, Köfte, Çiğ köfte, Manti,
Pide, Lahmacun, Menemen, Yaprak Sarma, Dolma,
İmam Bayıldı, Borek, Durum, Kumpir, Şiş Kebap,
Kebab Iskender, Kestane şekeri and Bak Mozavaik

SPORT
Soccer, Basketball and Volleyball

TOP 5 FAMOUS ATTRACTIONS
Ölüdeniz Blue Lagoon, Pamukkale, Ephesus, The
Maiden's Tower, Kas and Kalkan

Great Britain

Scotland

North Sea

Glasgow

Edinburgh Castle

Northern Ireland

Ireland

Liver Pool

Manchester

Irish Sea

London

England

Wales

White Cliffs of Dover

Celtic Sea

English Channel

UK
Hello!

CAPITAL
London

MUSIC AND TRADITIONAL DANCE
Shanties, Jigs, Hornpipes and Morris Dance

FOOD
Fish and Chips, Yorkshire Pudding, Full English Breakfast, Bangers and Mash, Shepherd's Pie or Cottage Pie, Steak and Kidney Pie, Beef Wellington, Afternoon Tea and Sticky Toffee Pudding

SPORT
Soccer, Rugby and Cricket

TOP 5 FAMOUS ATTRACTIONS
Westminster Palace, Big Ben Tower, London Bridge, Buckingham Palace and Windsor Castle

Germany
Hallo!

CAPITAL
Berlin

MUSIC AND TRADITIONAL DANCE
Polka and Tyrolean Dance

FOOD
Bratwurst, Schnitzel, Cordon Bleu, Maultaschen,
Klöße, Kartoffelsalat, Elbow with Chucrut, Brezel,
Berliner and Schwarzwälder Kirschtorte

SPORT
Soccer, Basketball and Auto Racing

TOP 5 FAMOUS ATTRACTIONS
Berlin Wall, Brandenburg Gate, Museum Island,
Neuschwanstein Castle and Colonia's cathedral

TRADE OF DIAMONDS

MANUFACTURE OF BILLIARD BALLS

FRENCH FRIES

BRUSSELS

THE CAPITAL OF THE EU

RAILROAD

ARC DE TRIOMPHE

BELFORT

BELGIUM

FLAG

MAP

BEER

POPPY

BICYCLE

WOMAN COSTUME

TRIUMPHAL ARCH

FOOTBALL

FRENCH FRIES

ATOMIUM

JENEVER

MOULES

STATUE

TOWER

DIAMOND

CHEESE

CASTLE

SYRUP

MAN COSTUME

WAFFLES

CROISSANT

CHOCOLATE

SYMBOL

GIN

HOUSE

Belgium
Salut!

CAPITAL
Brussels

MUSIC AND TRADITIONAL DANCE
The Zarda or Czarda

FOOD
Gulasch, Lángos, Palacsinta, Főzelék, Pörkölt, Gesztenyepüré, Somlói Galuska and Halászlé

SPORT
Soccer, Water Sports and Tennis

TOP 5 FAMOUS ATTRACTIONS
Balaton Lake, Buda Castle, Hortobágy National Park, Esztergom Basilica and The Aggtelek Caves

WINDMILLS

AMSTERDAM

BRIDGES

COFFEESHOPS

BICYCLISTS

EDAM CHEESE

ART

TULIPS

HERRING

= NETHERLANDS

AMSTERDAM

Netherlands
Hallo Daar!

CAPITAL
Amsterdam

MUSIC AND TRADITIONAL DANCE
Folkcorn and klompendans

FOOD
Poffertjes, Rookworst, Bitterballen, Appelflap,
Kroketten, Stamppot and Stroopwafels

SPORT
Soccer, Hockey and Volleyball

TOP 5 FAMOUS ATTRACTIONS
Kubuswoning Cube House, The Mills of Kinderdijk,
Anne Frank Museum, Van Gogh Museum and
The Canals of Amsterdam

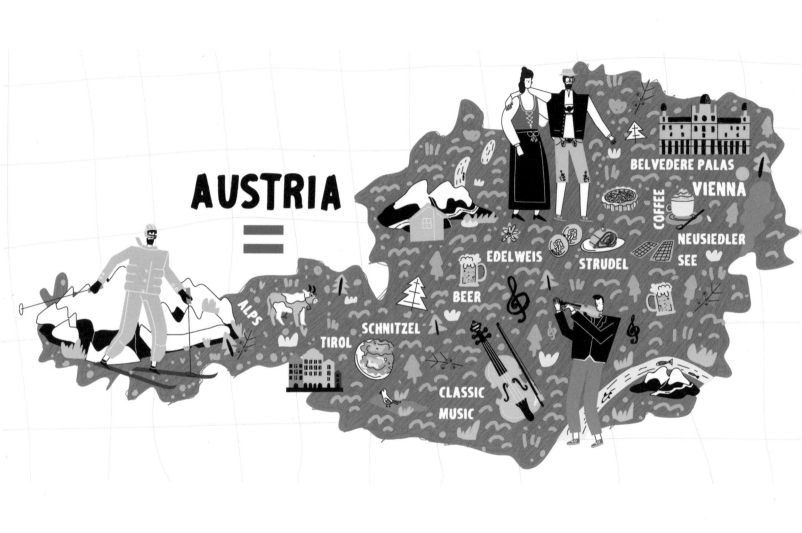

AUSTRIA

=

ALPS

TIROL

SCHNITZEL

CLASSIC MUSIC

EDELWEIS

BEER

STRUDEL

BELVEDERE PALAS

VIENNA

COFFEE

NEUSIEDLER SEE

Austria
Hallo!

CAPITAL
Vienna

MUSIC AND TRADITIONAL DANCE
Volksmusik and Vals

FOOD
Viennese Schnitzel, Vienna Sausage, Knödel, Tafelspitz, Tiroler Gröstl, Käsespätzle and Viennese Apfelstrudel

SPORT
Soccer, Alpine Skiing and Ice Hockey

TOP 5 FAMOUS ATTRACTIONS
Schönbrunn, Belvedere and Hofburg Palaces, St. Stephen's Cathedral and Hohensalzburg Fortress

Sopron

Budapest

Paprika

Hungary

Pécs

Hungary
Szia!

CAPITAL
Budapest

MUSIC AND TRADITIONAL DANCE
The Zarda or Czarda

FOOD
Gulasch, Lángos, Palacsinta, Főzelék, Pörkölt, Gesztenyepüré, Somlói Galuska and Halászlé.

SPORT
Soccer, Water Sports and Tennis

TOP 5 FAMOUS ATTRACTIONS
Balaton Lake, Buda Castle, Hortobágy National Park, Esztergom Basilica and The Aggtelek Caves

Serbia
Zdravo!

CAPITAL
Belgrade

MUSIC AND TRADITIONAL DANCE
Novokomponovana, Turbo-folk and Kolo

FOOD
Sarma, Ćevapi, Pljeskavica, Burek, Prebranac,
Punjena Paprika and Gibanica

SPORT
Soccer, Water polo and Basketball

TOP 5 FAMOUS ATTRACTIONS
The Monument of Stevan Sremac and Kalca,
The Belgrade Fortress, Kalemegdan Park,
St. Sava Temple and Knez Mihailova

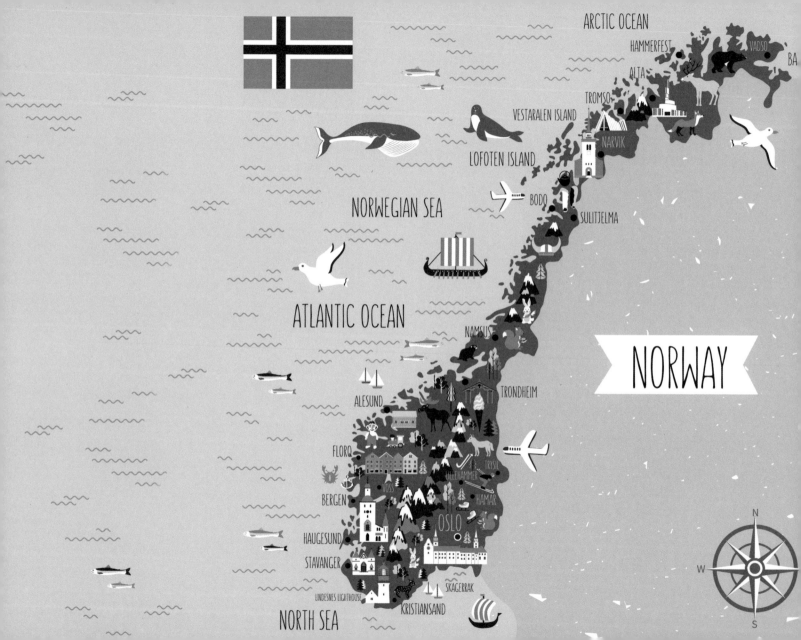

ARCTIC OCEAN

HAMMERFEST

VADSO

ALTA

BA

TROMSO

NARVIK

VESTARALEN ISLAND

LOFOTEN ISLAND

BODO

SULITJELMA

NORWEGIAN SEA

ATLANTIC OCEAN

NAMSUS

TRONDHEIM

NORWAY

ALESUND

FLORO

TRYSIL

LILLEHAMMER

VOSS

HAMAR

BERGEN

OSLO

HAUGESUND

STAVANGER

SKAGERRAK

LINDESNES LIGHTHOUSE

KRISTIANSAND

NORTH SEA

N

W

S

Norway
Hei!

CAPITAL
Oslo

MUSIC AND TRADITIONAL DANCE
Halling and Springar

FOOD
Fårikål, Kjøttkaker, Rakfish, Lefse, Kumla, Sodd,
Lapskaus, Brunost and Krumkake

SPORT
Skiing, Soccer and Auto Racing

TOP 5 FAMOUS ATTRACTIONS
The Fjord of Dreams, The Sognefjorden,
Jostedalsbreen, The Flåmsbana and
Nidaros Cathedral

DENMARK

WHALE

LINER

BAKING

KITE BUGGY

145

WHALE

CONSTRUCTOR

MERMAID

COPENHAGEN

COPENHAGEN

Denmark
Hej!

CAPITAL
Copenhagen

MUSIC AND TRADITIONAL DANCE
The Pols, Hopsa and Rheinlaender

FOOD
The Smørrebrød, The Flæskesteg, The Gravad
Laks, The Frikadeller, The Svineorbrad, The Sild,
The kraasesuppe Melbolle, The Hvid Labskovs, The
Akvavit and The Wienerbrød

SPORT
Soccer, Handball and Badminton

TOP 5 FAMOUS ATTRACTIONS
Copenhagen's Little Mermaid, Roskilde
Cathedral, Tivoli Gardens, Wadden Sea National
Park and Nyhavn

WELCOME TO
SWEDEN

STOCKHOLM

Sweden
Hej!

CAPITAL
Stockholm

MUSIC AND TRADITIONAL DANCE
Yodel and Ländler

FOOD
Rösti, Raclette, Carac, Fondue, Birchermüesli,
Saffron Risotto, Zürcher Geschnetzeltes, Zopf

SPORT
Ice Hockey, Soccer and Motorcycle Sports

TOP 5 FAMOUS ATTRACTIONS
Chillon Castle, Gruyères Medieval Castle, Bern
Clock Tower, The Fraumünster Church in Zurich,
The Chapel Bridge of Lucerne and Basel museums

Iceland
Halló!

CAPITAL
Reykjavik

MUSIC AND TRADITIONAL DANCE
Kveða, Syngja and Víkivaki

FOOD
Plokkfiskur, Hjónabandssæla, Kjötsúpa, Skyr,
Rúgbrauð, Kleinur, Harðfiskur, Pylsa, Lobster Soup,
Pönnukökur, and Hákarl

SPORT
Soccer, Basketball and Weightlifting

TOP 5 FAMOUS ATTRACTIONS
Hallgrímskirkja Church, Hofdi House, Reykjavik
Old Port, the Golden Circle and Gullfoss

KIEV

Ukraine
Pryvit!

CAPITAL
Kiev

MUSIC AND TRADITIONAL DANCE
Chant Rospiv, The Kozak and The Hopak

FOOD
Kholodets (meat or fish jelly), Borsch (beetroot soup), Paska (Ukrainian easter bread), Salo (pork fat), Holubtsi (stuffed cabbage leaves), Kovbasa (Ukrainian sausage), Varenyky (Ukrainian dumplings) and Potato pancakes

SPORT
Soccer, Athletics and Boxing

TOP 5 FAMOUS ATTRACTIONS
Frankvisk Oblast, St. Michael's Golden Domed Monastery, Askania-Nova Biosphere Reserve, Mount Hoverla and Chornohora

Russia
Privet!

CAPITAL
Moscow

MUSIC AND TRADITIONAL DANCE
Kadril, Trepak, Kalinka and Chechotka

FOOD
Shchi, Stroganoff, Shashlik, Pelmeni and Ukha

SPORT
Soccer, Basketball and Ice Hockey

TOP 5 FAMOUS ATTRACTIONS
Red Square, Saint Basil's Cathedral, Church of
the Savior on Blood, Peterhof Palace and Kazan
Cathedral

FINLAND

MOLOTOV COCTAIL

GINGER COOKIES

HEAVY MUSIC

AIR QUITAR CHAMPIONSHIP

BABY BOX

BASEBALL

SAUNAS

HELSINKI

HOCKEY

SANTA CLAUS

HELSINKI

Finland
Hei siellä!

CAPITAL
Helsinki

MUSIC AND TRADITIONAL DANCE
Karelia, Kantele, Kalevala, Polkka, Jenkka and Sottiisi

FOOD
Ruisleipä or Rye Bread, Porkkanat, Punajuuri,
Poro, Salmon, Karjalanpiirakka, Korvapuusti and
Leipäjuusto Cheese Bread

SPORT
Pesäpallo, Cross-Country Skiing and Canoeing

TOP 5 FAMOUS ATTRACTIONS
Ralinginkuja, Koli National park, Paavolan Tammi,
Santa's Refuge and Aavasaksa

Baltic Sea

Gulf of Riga

Latvia

RIGA

Liepaja

Jurmala

Daugavpils

WAGTAIL

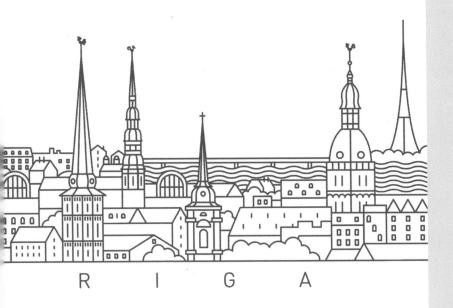

R I G A

Latvia
Sveiki!

CAPITAL
Riga

MUSIC AND TRADITIONAL DANCE
Dainas

FOOD
Rye Bread, Pīrāgi, Pelmeni, Smoked Fish,
Janu Cheese, Aukstā Zupa, Karbonāde and
Alexandertorte

SPORT
Soccer, Basketball and Bowling

TOP 5 FAMOUS ATTRACTIONS
Vecriga, Sigulda Medieval Castle, Gauja National
Park, Jurmala and Cape Kolka Slitere National Park

Welcome to Asia!

- Asia is the largest continent on the planet. And to top it off, it is also the most populated continent in the world.
- There are more than 2,300 recognized languages in Asia!
- The largest city is Tokyo.
- Japan has the longest life expectancy.
- Fourteen of the world's highest mountains can be found in Asia, all of which are more than 8,000 meters above sea level. The highest mountain in the world is Mount Everest, which stands at 8,848 meters.
- In the Asian continent you can see wild animals, tigers, snow leopards, orangutans and some of the most venomous snakes in the world.
- If you visit an Asian market, you are likely to find some "exotic" snacks. Silkworms are a popular snack in many countries, but you can also find fried crickets and other types of insects.

- Asia es el continente más grande del planeta, y, por si fuera poco, también es el continente más poblado del mundo.
- ¡Hay más de 2300 idiomas reconocidos!.
- La ciudad más grande es Tokio.
- Japón tiene la mayor esperanza de vida.
- 14 de las montañas más altas del mundo se pueden encontrar en Asia, estando todas ellas a más de 8.000 metros sobre el nivel del mar. La montaña más alta del mundo es el Monte Everest, que está a 8.848 metros.
- En el continente asiático puedes ver animales salvajes, tigres, leopardos de las nieves, orangutanes y algunas de las serpientes más venenosas del mundo.
- Si visitas un mercado asiático, es probable que encuentres algunos snacks "exóticos". Los gusanos de seda son un aperitivo popular en muchos países, pero también puedes encontrar grillos y otros tipos de insectos fritos.

NORTH

China
Ni hao!

CAPITAL
Beijing

MUSIC AND TRADITIONAL DANCE
Youlan 'or the Lonely Orchid, Dragon dance and
Lion dance

FOOD
Shark Fin Soup, Zongzi, Dim Sum, Wonton,
Abalone, Chicken Gong Bao, Chop Suey,
Lacquered Duck, Huo Guo, Fortune Cookies and
Pineapple Buns

SPORT
Table Tennis, Badminton and Tai Chi

TOP 5 FAMOUS ATTRACTIONS
The Great Wall, The Forbidden City in Beijing, The
Li River in Guilin, The Yellow Mountains and The
Potala Palace of TibetPark, Jurmala and Cape Kolka
Slitere National Park

Welcome to Taiwan

KEELUNG

TAIPEI

YILAN

TAICHUNG

NANTOU

CHANGHUA

TAITUNG

TAINAN

PINGTUNG

Eat, drink and be merry!

Taiwan
Ni hao!

CAPITAL
Taipei

MUSIC AND TRADITIONAL DANCE
Nanguan and Eight Generals Dance

FOOD
Beef Noodle Soup, XiaoLongBao, Pearl Milk Tea, Oyster Omelette, Braised Pork Rice, Fried Squid, Stinky Tofu and Oyster pancakes

SPORT
Taekwondo, Baseball and Table Tennis

TOP 5 FAMOUS ATTRACTIONS
National Palace Museum, Maokong, Taroko Gorge, Kaohsiung, Green Island

Hong Kong
Néi Hóu!

CAPITAL
Hong Kong

MUSIC AND TRADITIONAL DANCE
The Lion and the Dragon Dance

FOOD
Roast Goose, Char Siu, Wonton Noodle Soup, Naai
Caa, Yuanyang, Egg Waffle and Fish balls

SPORT
Dragon Regattas, Rugby and Soccer

TOP 5 FAMOUS ATTRACTIONS
Big Buddha, Victoria Peak, Tsim Sha Tsui, Lantau
island and Sai Kung

South Korea
Annyeonghaseyo!

CAPITAL
Seoul

MUSIC AND TRADITIONAL DANCE
Gugak, Yangak, Salpurichum, Gutchum,
Taepyeongmu, Buchaechum and Geommu

FOOD
Kimchi, Bibimbap, Kimbap, Bulgogi, Tteokbokki,
Jajangmyeon and Samgyeopsal

SPORT
Ssireum, Taekwondo and Soccer

TOP 5 FAMOUS ATTRACTIONS
Hwaseong Fortress, Gayasan Mountain Haeinsa
Temple, Haedong Yonggungsa Temple, Busan
Jagalchi Market and Jeju Island

WELCOME TO JAPAN

日本の旅

Japan
Kon'nichiwa!

CAPITAL
Tokyo

MUSIC AND TRADITIONAL DANCE
Hougaku, Mai, Odori and Shosa

FOOD
Sushi, Onigiri, Ramen, Udon and Soba, Gyudon,
Tonkatsu and Katsudon, Tempura, Sashami, Teriyaki,
Bento and Mochis

SPORT
Sumo, Kendo and Karate

TOP 5 FAMOUS ATTRACTIONS
Tokyo, Nikko, Kamakura, Kyoto and Osaka

Vietnam

Xin Chào!

CAPITAL
Hanoi

MUSIC AND TRADITIONAL DANCE
Thang Long, Gay, La Luc Cung or La Thien Long
Bat Boo

FOOD
Pho, Goi Cuon, Cau Lao, Bun Cha, Hotpot, Banh
Mi, Banh Xeo and Won Ton

SPORT
Soccer, Jianzi or Shuttlecock and Taekwondo

TOP 5 FAMOUS ATTRACTIONS
Halong Bay, Sapa Mountains, Ban Gioc Falls,
Hanoi Old Town and Hue Imperial City

WAT PHRA THAT
DOI SUTHEP

SAO CHINGCHA

PHANOM RUNG
HISTORICAL PARK

WAT ARUN RATCHAWARARAM

WAT PHRA KAEW

PATTAYA

KOH PHANGAN

PHUKET

Thailand
Swasdi!

CAPITAL
Bangkok

MUSIC AND TRADITIONAL DANCE
Luk Thung and Mor Lam, khon, Li-khe, Ram Wong, Shadow Puppets, Lakhon Lek and Lakhon

FOOD
Pad Thai, Som Tam, Khao Pad Saparod, Kai Pad Med Mamuang, Pad Krapau, Pad Siuw, Kai Tod, Kuai Tieow, Yam Ma Khwa Yao, Kai and Mu Satae

SPORT
Muay Thai, Sepak Takraw and Badminton

TOP 5 FAMOUS ATTRACTIONS
Railay Beach, Damnoen Saduak Floating Market, Pai Canyon, Khao Yai National Park and Ayutthaya Historic City

Cambodia
Sau Stei!

CAPITAL
Phnom Penh

MUSIC AND TRADITIONAL DANCE
Apsara, Romvong and Lam Vong

FOOD
Amok, K'tieu, Bai Saik Ch'rouk, Lok Lak, Chok Nom Bahn, Chaa Kdam, Prahok, Lap Khmer, Khmer Red Curry and Tuk-a-Loc

SPORT
Prodal or Khmer Boxing, Soccer and Volleyball

TOP 5 FAMOUS ATTRACTIONS
Mondulkiri, Phnom Penh, Preah Vihear Temple, Ream National Park and Siem Reap Temples

MALAYSIA

Malaysia
Halo!

CAPITAL
Kuala Lumpur

MUSIC AND TRADITIONAL DANCE
Zapin, Ghazal, Dondang Sayang, Mata-kantiga,
Joget and Bangsawan

FOOD
Nasi lemak, Satay, Ketupat, Wanton Mee, Nasi
Goreng, Roti canai, and Murtabak

SPORT
Soccer, Auto Racing and Pencak Silat

TOP 5 FAMOUS ATTRACTIONS
Perhentian Islands, Langkawi, Titiwangsa
Mountains, Malacca and Kota Bharu

Singapore
Ni Hao!

CAPITAL
Singapore

MUSIC AND TRADITIONAL DANCE
Karnatic, Bhangra and Chinese Lion Dance

FOOD
Hainan Chicken Rice, Hokkien Prawn Mee, Wanton Mee, Tau Huey, Dim Sum, Chai Tow Kway, Congee with Frog, Roti Prata, Char Kway Teow, Nasi Lemak, Laksa and Spicy Crab

SPORT
Soccer, Rugby and Water Sports

TOP 5 FAMOUS ATTRACTIONS
Gardens by the Bay, Clarke Quay, Hawkers, Peranakan Terrace Houses and Sentosa Island

Paoay Church

Luzon

Manila

Mayon Volcano

Mindoro

Samar

Boracay

Panay

Cebu

Leyte

Palawan

Mindanao

Davao

Philippines

Kamusta Po Diyan!

CAPITAL
Manila

MUSIC AND TRADITIONAL DANCE
Gong music, Kulintang, Tinikling, Maglalatik, Binasuan and Pantomina

FOOD
Ginataang Isda Kalabasa, Pancit Bihon, Pork Sinigang, Pork Adobo, Tinolang Manok, Filipino Chicken Macaroni Soups, Lumpiang, Longaniza, Halo-halo and Banana Nougat

SPORT
Basketball, Badminton and Boxing

TOP 5 FAMOUS ATTRACTIONS
Chocolate Hills, Tubbataha Reefs, Mount Mayon, Banaue Rice Terraces and Donsol

Indonesia
Halo!

CAPITAL
Jakarta

MUSIC AND TRADITIONAL DANCE
Gamelan

FOOD
Nasi Campur, Nasi Goreng, Mee Goreng, Sate
(or Satay), Gado Gado, Lumpia, Bakso, Kari Ayam,
Pepes Ikan and Pisang Goreng

SPORT
Badminton, Soccer and Sepak Takraw

TOP 5 FAMOUS ATTRACTIONS
Lake Toba, Tanjung National Park, Bunaken,
Borobudur Buddhist Temple, Bali and Java

Nepal
Namaskar!

CAPITAL
Kathmandu

MUSIC AND TRADITIONAL DANCE
Tamang Selo, Chyabrung, Dohori, Adhunik Geet, Bhajan, Filmi music, Ghazal and Tandava Dance

FOOD
Dal Bhat, Thenthuk, Tsampa, Momos, Thukpa, Sha-Balé, Kongpo Shaptak, Mar Jasha and Shamday

SPORT
Volleyball, Dandi Biyo and Kabaddi

TOP 5 FAMOUS ATTRACTIONS
Everest, Bhaktapur, Nagarkot, Pokhara Valley and Chitwan National Park

India

Namaste!

CAPITAL
New Delhi

MUSIC AND TRADITIONAL DANCE
Dhrupad, Dhamar, Khyal, Tarana and Sadra,
Bharata Natyam, Kathakali, Mohini Attam,
Odissi, Kuchipudi, Kathak and Manipuri

FOOD
Lamb Tikka Masala, Chicken Vindaloo, Samosas,
Masala Dosa, Naan, Chole Bhature, Tandoori
Chicken, Palak Paneer, Lassi, El Biryani, Balti
Curries, Daal Tarka and Rajma

SPORT
Cricket, Kabaddi and Field Hockey

TOP 5 FAMOUS ATTRACTIONS
Taj Mahal, Varanasi, Ajanta Caves, Jaisalmer and
Kanha National Park

Sri Lanka
Eyi Me!

CAPITAL
Sri Jayawardenapura Kotte

MUSIC AND TRADITIONAL DANCE
Kavi, Virindu, Rata Natum, Pahatha Rata Natum
and Sabaragamuwa

FOOD
Roti, Kottu, Egg Hopper, Biryani, Fish Ambul Thiyal,
Lamprais, Kukul Mas Curry and Kokis

SPORT
Volleyball, Cricket and Rugby

TOP 5 FAMOUS ATTRACTIONS
Polonnaruwa, Ella, Minneriya National Park,
Dambulla Caves and Anuradhapura

United Arab Emirates

Dubai Gold Souk

Al Badiyah Mosque

Jumeirah Mosque

Sheikh Zayed Grand Mosque

Dubai Museum

Al Jahili Fort

Jebel Hafeet

UAE
Marhaban!

CAPITAL
Abu Dhabi

MUSIC AND TRADITIONAL DANCE
Liwa, Ayyalah, Raqs Sarqi and Al Ayyala

FOOD
Blakawa, Chai Zan-Ja- Beel, Kebbe Naie,
Le-ge- Matt, Massaf, Arabic Mezze, Mutabal
and Arabic Tabbouleh

SPORT
Soccer, Endurance Riding and Camel Racing

TOP 5 FAMOUS ATTRACTIONS
Burj Khalifa and Bastakia neighborhood of Dubai,
Sheikh Zayed Mosque, Hajar Mountains, Jebel
Hafeet and Al Bidya Mosque

Welcome to Africa!

- With a land area of 30,370,000 square kilometers, Africa is the second largest continent on the planet. Only Asia is more extensive, based on total area.
- More than 2,000 languages are spoken in Africa.
- Algeria is the largest African country.
- Women and children walk an average of 5.9 km every day just to get the water they need to survive. The way they carry heavy buckets of water (carrying them on their heads) has become famous around the world.
- It is a continent full of natural heritage sites, but there are also those created by man. The most famous is the Great Pyramid of Giza, which is the only remaining monument of the seven ancient wonders of the world.
- Africa has the largest desert in the world, the Sahara. It also has the longest river in the world, the Nile.

- Con una superficie terrestre de 30.370.000 km2, África es el segundo continente más grande del planeta. Solo Asia es más extensa, según la superficie total.
- Se hablan alrededor de 2.000 lenguas.
- Argelia es el país africano más grande.
- Las mujeres y los niños andan una media de 5,9 km cada día solo para conseguir el agua que necesitan para sobrevivir, la forma en la que cargan pesados cubos de agua (llevándolos sobre su cabeza) se ha hecho famosa en todo el mundo.
- Es un continente lleno de sitios que son patrimonio natural, pero también destacan los creados por el hombre. El más famoso es, la Gran Pirámide de Guiza, que es el único monumento que queda de las siete antiguas maravillas del mundo.
- África tiene el mayor desierto del mundo, el Sahara, también tiene el río más largo del mundo, el Nilo.

NORTH

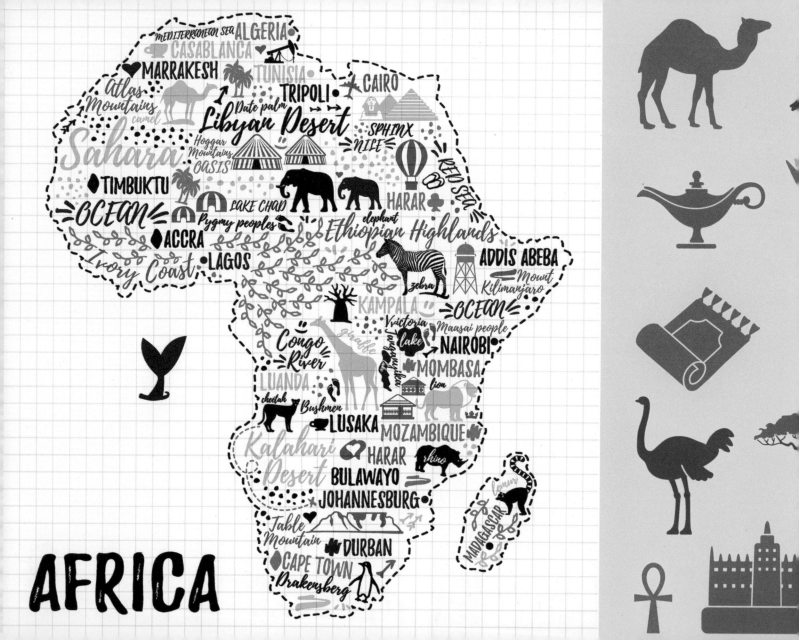

Kenya
Habari!

CAPITAL
Nairobi

MUSIC AND TRADITIONAL DANCE
Traditional Kenyan Tribal Dances

FOOD
Nyama Choma, Ugali, Tilapia, Sukuma Wiki,
Pilau, Matoke, Githeri, Samosas, Maharagwe
and Matumbo

SPORT
Athletics, Soccer and Cricket

TOP 5 FAMOUS ATTRACTIONS
Masai Mara National Park, Karen Blixen's House,
Lamu, Lake Nakuru and Amboseli National Park

Mediterranean Sea
Marsa
Alexandria
N
W
E
S
Siwah
Cairo
Giza
EGYPT
Sinai
Asyut
Hurghada
Suhaj
Qina
Luxor
Al Kharjah
Mut
Red Sea
Kom ombo
Abu Sunbul

Egypt
Marhaban!

CAPITAL
Cairo

MUSIC AND TRADITIONAL DANCE
Fallah, Saidi, Nubia and Belly Dance

FOOD
Ful Medames, Koshari, Baba Ganoush, Fatteh,
Kofta, Mulukhiyah, Mahshi, Baklava, Kanafeh,
Falafel and Shawarma

SPORT
Soccer, Basketball and Handball

TOP 5 FAMOUS ATTRACTIONS
Pyramids of Giza, Valley of the Kings, Karnak
Temples, Abu Simbel and Siwa

FEZ, MOROCCO

Morocco
Marhaban!

CAPITAL
Rabat

MUSIC AND TRADITIONAL DANCE
Andalusian Music, El Hait, Shikat Belly Dance and Barbari Dance

FOOD
Couscous, Hummus, Tajine, Pastilla, Bissara, Harira, Kefta, Touajen and Hout, Eggplant Zaalouk, Méchoui and Djaja Mahamara

SPORT
Soccer, Auto Racing and Equestrian Sports

TOP 5 FAMOUS ATTRACTIONS
Chefchaouen, Erg Chebbi, Draa Valley, Meknes and Djemaa el Fna

Welcome to
North America!

North America is made up of only three countries (Canada, USA and Mexico), but it lacks nothing: big cities, rolling prairies, rugged mountains, giant forests, magnificent beaches, arid deserts, arctic cold and much more. It is an authentic meeting place and confluence of multiple cultures from all corners of the world. It is if the world had been compressed into a single large continent.

Norteamérica está compuesta únicamente por tres países (Canadá, USA y México), pero no le falta de nada: grandes ciudades, onduladas praderas, escarpadas montañas, gigantes bosques, fastuosas playas, áridos desiertos, frío ártico y mucho más. Se trata de un auténtico lugar de encuentro y confluencia de múltiples culturas de todos los rincones. Como si el mundo se hubiera comprimido en un único continente de gran tamaño.

Canada
Hello!

CAPITAL
Ottawa

MUSIC AND TRADITIONAL DANCE
Red River Jig

FOOD
Fiddleheads, Montreal Bagels, Poutine,
Sándwich Boeuf Fumé, Calgary Beef Hash,
Peameal Bacon and Tourtiere

SPORT
Ice Hockey, Basketball and Lacrosse

TOP 5 FAMOUS ATTRACTIONS
Niagara Falls, Valley of the Ten Peaks, Bay of
Fundy, Capilano Suspension Bridge and Dinosaur
Provincial Park

USA

The United States is made up of 50 states occupying more than 9 million square kilometers. It has a population of over 320 million people!
The flag of the United States has been modified on numerous occasions. The current one was created by Robert G. Heft, a 17-year-old student, as an assignment for history class. "In God We Trust," the current motto of the United States was chosen in 1956, and this inscription appears on all coins and dollar bills. When measured from the base of the ocean, the dormant volcano Mauna Kea in Hawaii surpasses Everest.
The State of Wyoming was a pioneer of women's suffrage. As such, it was also the first state to have a female governor in 1924: Nellie Tayloe Ross. American universities top the world rankings. Harvard being in the number 1 position. As far as sports are concerned, since the 1990s American soccer has overtaken baseball. The Super Bowl is a defining moment for the country, both culturally and economically.
It is a country that has no official language at the federal level, although 80% of the population speaks English. The second most spoken language is Spanish, at 13%. Some 20 million Americans live in mobile homes.

Estados Unidos está formado por 50 estados ocupando más de 9 millones de kilómetros cuadrados. ¡Tiene una población de más de 320 millones de personas! La bandera de Estados Unidos ha sido modificada en numerosas ocasiones. La actual fué creada por Robert G. Heft, un estudiante de 17 años, como trabajo para la clase de historia. "In God We Trust", el actual lema de Estados Unidos se eligió en 1956, y esta inscripción aparece en todas las monedas y billetes de dólares. Si se mide desde la base del océano, el volcán inactivo Mauna Kea, en Hawaii, supera al Everest. El Estado de Wyoming fue pionero con el voto femenino. Por eso, también fue el primer estado en tener una gobernadora en 1924: Nellie Tayloe Ross Las universidades americanas ocupan y encabezan los rankings mundiales. Siendo el puesto número 1 para Harvard. En lo que a deporte se refiere, desde los años 90 el fútbol americano ha desbancado al béisbol. La Super Bowl, es todo un momento crucial para el país, tanto cultural como económicamente. Es un país que no tiene idioma oficial a nivel federal, si bien el 80% de la población habla inglés. El segundo idioma más hablado es el español, con el 13%.
Unos 20 millones de estadounidenses viven en casas móviles.

PENSACOLA

APALACHICOLA

TALLAHASEE

JACKSONVILLE

FLORIDA

ORLANDO

TAMPA

SARASOTA

CAPE CANNAVERAL

GULF OF MEXICO

EVER GLADES

MIAMI

KEY WEST

FLORIDA KEYS

Florida
Hello!

CAPITAL
Tallahassee

MUSIC AND TRADITIONAL DANCE
Southern Rap, Latin music, Electronic and
Rock music

FOOD
Key Lime Pie, Conch Fritters, Apachicola
Oysters, Gator Tail, Fried Gator and Smoked fish

SPORT
American Football, Basketball and Golf

TOP 5 FAMOUS ATTRACTIONS
Kennedy Space Center, Ocean Drive, Florida Keys,
Walt Disney World and Key West

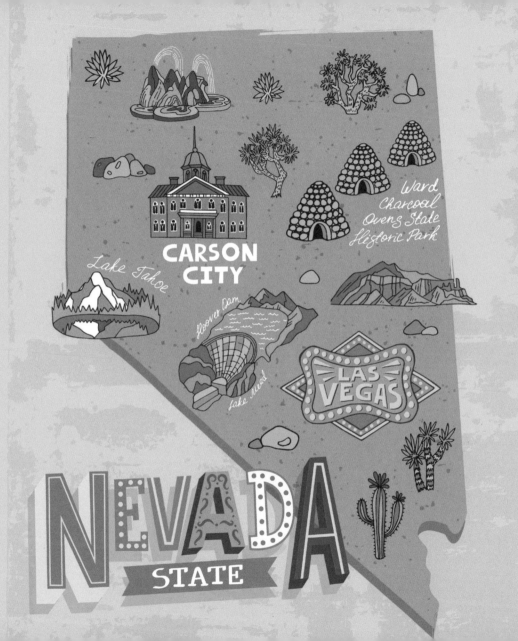

CARSON
CITY

Lake Tahoe

Ward
Charcoal
Ovens State
Historic Park

Hoover Dam

Lake Mead

LAS
VEGAS

NEVADA
STATE

Nevada
Hello!

CAPITAL
Carson City

MUSIC AND TRADITIONAL DANCE
Alt-rock, Pop and Lounge

FOOD
Miso-Glazed Chilean Sea, Maine-Style Lobster Roll,
Cannoli and Chicken 'N' Watermelon 'N' Waffles

SPORT
Ice Hockey, Basketball and Boxing

TOP 5 FAMOUS ATTRACTIONS
Red Rock Canyon National Conservation Area,
Las Vegas Strip, Hoover Dam, Grapevine Canyon
Petroglyphs and Valley of Fire State Park

Adirondack mountains

Lake Champlain

Lake George

NIAGARA FALLS

LAKE ONTARIO

Rochester

Seneca Lake

Cayuga Lake

Syracuse

Albany

Hudson River

New York

NEW YORK [S] [STATE]

Long Island

New York
Hello!

CAPITAL
Albany

MUSIC AND TRADITIONAL DANCE
Jazz, Hip Hop and Rock music

FOOD
Hot Dog, Bagel, Pretzel and Bubba Gump

SPORT
Basketball, American Football and Baseball

TOP 5 FAMOUS ATTRACTIONS
Central Park, Statue of Liberty, Empire State
Building, Times Square and Brooklyn Bridge

Oregon
Hello!

CAPITAL
Salem

MUSIC AND TRADITIONAL DANCE
Rock & Roll, Country and Rhythm & Blues.
FOOD: Smoked Pacific salmon, Chanterelle and
Pok Pok Wings

FOOD
Basketball, American Football and Golf

SPORT
Basketball, American Football and Baseball

TOP 5 FAMOUS ATTRACTIONS
Mount Hood, Umpqua National Forest,
Columbia River Gorge, Multnomah Falls and
Crater Lake National ParkBuilding,
Times Square and Brooklyn Bridge

Tennessee
illinois
Kentucky
missouri
virginia
Mississippi River
ROCK'N ROLL
Nashville
Knoxville
Memphis
Tennessee River
north carolina
south carolina
mississippi
alabama
georgia

Tennessee
Hello!

CAPITAL
Nashville

MUSIC AND TRADITIONAL DANCE
Country & Bluegrass

FOOD
Country Ham, BBQ, Cornbread and
Banana pudding

SPORT
Basketball, Hockey and American football

TOP 5 FAMOUS ATTRACTIONS
Broadway Honky Tonks, Cummins Falls,
Chattanooga, Great Smoky Mountains National
Park and Country Music Hall of Fame

Arizona
Hello!

CAPITAL
Phoenix

MUSIC AND TRADITIONAL DANCE
Alt-Rock, Pop and Country music

FOOD
Sonoran Hot Dog, Red Chile Stew and Tamales

SPORT
Basketball, American Football and Baseball

TOP 5 FAMOUS ATTRACTIONS
Monument Valley, Grand Canyon, Horseshoe
Bend, Oak Creek Canyon and Watson Lake

Sassafras Mtn 3560

Blue Ridge

ROCK HILL

Carolina Wren

Columbia

Myrtle Beach

South Carolina

Hilton head island

Charleston

SOUTH CAROLINA

South Carolina

Hello!

CAPITAL
Columbia

MUSIC AND TRADITIONAL DANCE
Soul and Rhythm & Blues

FOOD
Collard Greens, Frogmore Stew, Chicken Bog,
Oyster Roast and Boiled Peanuts

SPORT
American Football, Ice Hockey and Golf

TOP 5 FAMOUS ATTRACTIONS
Charleston, Caesars Head, Hilton Head Island,
Congaree National Park and Myrtle Beach

SAN FRANCISCO

California

Hello!

CAPITAL
Sacramento

MUSIC AND TRADITIONAL DANCE
Surf & Psychedelic Rock and Bakersfield Sound

FOOD
Cheeseburger, Burrito, Avocado Toast
and Cobb Salad

SPORT
Basketball, American Football and Soccer

TOP 5 FAMOUS ATTRACTIONS
Yosemite National Park, Death Valley,
San Bernardino Forest, Kings Canyon and
Sequoia National Park

DA

Niagara
Falls

New
York

Atlantic
Ocean

Glacier National Park
Flathead Lake
MISSOULA
GLASGOW
GREAT FALLS
Missouri River
HELENA
BILLINGS
Yellowstone River
ROCKY MOUNTAINS
MONTANA

MINNESOTA
Lake Superior
MICH
MILK
BEER
IOWA
Milwaukee
Madison
WISCONSIN

OKLAHOMA
ROUTE 66
TULSA
OKLAHOMA CITY

YELLOW STONE NATIONAL PARK
DEVILS TOWER
GRAND TETON
GILLETTE
JACKSON
CASPER
Wyoming
CHEYENNE

SPRINGFIELD
Quabbin Reservoir
CAMBRIDGE
WORCESTER
BOSTON
cape Cod
Welcome to
MASSACHUSETTS
FALL RIVER
Buzzards Bay

Mexico
¡Hola!

CAPITAL
Ciudad de Mexico

MUSIC AND TRADITIONAL DANCE
Huapango, Ranchera, Corrido, Vals and
Son Huasteco

FOOD
Tacos, Fajitas, Quesadilla, Enchilada, Totopos,
Mole and Tamales

SPORT
Soccer, Basketball and Baseball

TOP 5 FAMOUS ATTRACTIONS
Chichen Itza, Palenque, Calakmul Biosphere
Reserve, Tulum and Punta Cometa Peninsula

Welcome to
South America!

- Many great civilizations have lived here. The Incas may be the most famous civilization, as their empire extended over much of South America.
- Many of the ancient sites are still preserved today, of which Machu Picchu is the most famous.
- South America has an immense musical culture, and is the cradle of dance styles such as samba, mambo, tango, among many others.
- The Amazon Rainforest is the most biodiverse place in the world, containing more than 40% of the world's plants and animals.
- La Paz, the Bolivian capital, has an elevation of 3,640 meters (11,942 feet), making it one of the highest cities in the world.
- Brazil is the largest country in South America. At the other extreme, Suriname holds the title of the continent's smallest country.
- The highest mountain in South America is known as Aconcagua and rises majestically 6,962 meters above sea level in Argentina.
- Venezuela's Angel Falls is the highest waterfall in the world. It boasts the impressive height of... 979 meters!

- Muchas grandes civilizaciones han vivido aquí, puede que los Incas sean la civilización más famosa, ya que su imperio se extendía por gran parte de Sudamérica.
- Todavía hoy se conservan muchos de los sitios antiguos, de los cuales el Machu Picchu es el más famoso.
- Sudamérica posee una cultura musical inmensa, y es la cuna de estilos de bailes como la samba, el mambo, el tango, entre muchísimos otros.
- La Selva Amazónica es el lugar con más biodiversidad del mundo, conteniendo más del 40 % de las plantas y animales del mundo.
- La Paz, capital boliviana, tiene una elevación de 3.640 metros (11.942 pies), lo que la convierte en una de las ciudades con más altura del mundo.
- Brasil es el país más grande de Sudamérica, en el otro extremo, Surinam ostenta el título del país más pequeño del continente.
- La montaña más alta de Sudamérica es conocida como Aconcagua y se alza majestuosamente 6.962 metros por encima del nivel del mar en Argentina.
- El Salto del Ángel de Venezuela, es la cascada más alta del mundo, tiene la impresionante altura de... ¡979 metros!

 NORTH

EQUADOR

COLUMBIA

PACAYA SAMIRIA

PIURA

BRAZIL

KUELAP

PERU

HUACA HUALAMARCA

BOLIVIA

CUSCO

SAQSAYWAMAN

LIMA

PACIFIC OCEAN

CHILE

MACHUPICCHU

MISTI

Peru
¡Hola!

CAPITAL
Lima

MUSIC AND TRADITIONAL DANCE
Zamacueca, Pitita, Marinera, Huayno y Samba Land

FOOD
Ceviche, Chifa, Pachamanca and Peruvian curry

SPORT
Soccer, Baseball and Volleyball

TOP 5 FAMOUS ATTRACTIONS
Machu Picchu, Sacred Valley, Colca Canyon,
Chan Chan and The Huaca del Sol

Argentina
¡Hola!

CAPITAL
Buenos Aires

MUSIC AND TRADITIONAL DANCE
Tango

FOOD
Asado, Locro, Choripán, Empanadas and
Milanesa a la Napolitana

SPORT
Soccer, Basketball and Hockey

TOP 5 FAMOUS ATTRACTIONS
Iguazu Falls, Nahuel Huapi Lake, Patagonia,
Quebrada de Humahuaca and
The Hill of Seven Colors

Brazil
Olá!

CAPITAL
Brasilia

MUSIC AND TRADITIONAL DANCE
Samba, Bossa Nova, Chorinho and Frevo

FOOD
Feijoada, Vatapá, Acarajé and Picanha

SPORT
Soccer, Futsal and Beach Soccer

TOP 5 FAMOUS ATTRACTIONS
Corcovado, Lençóis Maranhenses National
Park, Fernando de Noronha Island, Sugarloaf
Mountain and Chapada Diamantina

TIME TO EXPLORE
CHILE

Chile
¡Hola!

CAPITAL
Santiago de Chile

MUSIC AND TRADITIONAL DANCE
Tonada, Canto and Cueca

FOOD
Charquicán, Caldillo de Congrio and Chochoca

SPORT
Soccer, Tennis and Polo

TOP 5 FAMOUS ATTRACTIONS
Rapa Nui National Park, Churches of
Chiloé, Sewell City, The Chilean Inca Trail,
Humberstone and Santa Laura Saltpeter Works

Cuba

¡Hola!

CAPITAL
La Habana

MUSIC AND TRADITIONAL DANCE
Danzón, Guaracha, Son cubano, Bolero, Mambo, Chachachá, Rumba and Guaguancó

FOOD
Ropa Vieja, Frijoles Negros Cubanos, Moros y Cristianos and Ajiaco

SPORT
Volleyball, Baseball and Boxing

TOP 5 FAMOUS ATTRACTIONS
Malecón, Viñales Valley, Saint Mary Cay, Trinidad City, and Varadero

Pacific Ocean

Galapagos Islands

Quito

Guayaquil

Ecuador

Cuenca

00°00'00"

Ecuador
¡Hola!

CAPITAL
Quito

MUSIC AND TRADITIONAL DANCE
Marimba, Amorfino and Sanjuanito

FOOD
Hornado, Fritada, Mote Pata and Encebollado

SPORT
Soccer, Boxing and Ice Hockey

TOP 5 FAMOUS ATTRACTIONS
Middle of the World City, Quilotoa, Basilica of
the National Vow, Galápagos National Park and
Tortuga Bay

OCEAN

Java

New Guinea

Kakadu
JIM JIM FALLS
DARVIN
Boomerang
Road Train

Cape York
Sugar-cane

Great Barrier Reef

OCEAN

Great Sandy Desert

platypus

wallaby

AYERS ROCK

ABORIGINAL

wallaroo

Whitsunday

Great Christmas Range

Budgerigar

kookaburra

FRASER ISLAND

echidna

sailboat

koala

Eucalyptus

Gibson Desert

Flinders Range

Great Victoria Desert

Simpson Desert

DINGO

QUEENSLANDER

BRISBANE

Harbour Bridge

PERT

KALGOORLIE

ALBANY

Great Australian Bight

Great Ocean Road

KANGAROO

Australian Alps

OPERA HOUSE

CANBERRA

Penguin Parade

SURFING

SEA

Bondi Beach

MELBOURNE

Dandenong Ranges

Phillip Island

NEW ZEALAND

Royal Regatta
HOBART

Welcome to Oceania!

• This amazing continent is located almost entirely in the Pacific. The largest countries on this continent are Australia, Papua New Guinea and New Zealand. They are also the most populated in the same order.
And the smallest ones are Nauru, Tuvalu and the Marshall Islands.
• The four languages with the largest number of native speakers in Oceania are English, Tok Pisin, French and Fijian Hindi.
• The Great Barrier Reef is the largest reef in the world, with some 3,000 individual reefs and 900 islands.
• Milford Fjord in New Zealand is known as the "eighth wonder of the world."

• Este asombroso continente se encuentra situado casi enteramente sobre la placa del Pacífico. Los mayores países de este continente son Australia, Papúa Nueva Guinea y Nueva Zelanda. También son los más poblados en el mismo orden. Y los más pequeños, Nauru, Tuvalu y las Islas Marshall.
• Las cuatro lenguas con mayor número de hablantes nativos en Oceanía son el inglés, el tok pisin, el francés y el hindi de Fiyi.
• La Gran Barrera de Coral es el arrecife más grande del mundo, cuenta con unos 3 mil arrecifes individuales y 900 islas.
• El Fiordo Milford en Nueva Zelanda es conocido como la «octava maravilla del mundo».

NORTH

AUSTRALIA

Australia

Hello!

CAPITAL
Canberra

MUSIC AND TRADITIONAL DANCE
Bush Dance

FOOD
Dog's Eye, Crocodile Meat, Barramundi
and Lamington

SPORT
Cricket, Australian Football and Hockey

TOP 5 FAMOUS ATTRACTIONS
Uluru-Kata Tjuta National Park, The Twelve
Apostles, Sydney Opera House, Bondi Beach
and Kakadu National Park

New Zealand
Kia Ora!

CAPITAL
Wellington

MUSIC AND TRADITIONAL DANCE
Haka

FOOD
Crayfish and seafood, Roast Lamb and Hāngī

SPORT
Rugby, Cricket and Netball

TOP 5 FAMOUS ATTRACTIONS
Fiordland National Park and Milford Sound,
Rotorua, Fox and Franz Josef Glaciers, Kaikoura,
Lake Taupo and Tongariro National Park